GRAPHIC BIOGRAPHIES

AMELIA EARHART
LEGENDARY AVIATOR

by Jameson Anderson
illustrated by Rod Whigham and
Charles Barnett III

Consultant:
Sammie Morris, Archivist
The George Palmer Putnam Collection of
Amelia Earhart Papers
Purdue University

Capstone
press®

Mankato, Minnesota

Graphic Library is published by Capstone Press,
151 Good Counsel Drive, P.O. Box 669, Mankato, Minnesota 56002.
www.capstonepress.com

Printed in the United States of America

1 2 3 4 5 6 11 10 09 08 07 06

Library of Congress Cataloging-in-Publication Data
Anderson, Jameson.
Amelia Earhart: legendary aviator / by Jameson Anderson; illustrated by Rod Whigham and Charles Barnett III.
p. cm.—(Graphic library. Graphic biographies)
Includes bibliographical references and index.
ISBN-13: 978-0-7368-6496-1 (hardcover)
ISBN-10: 0-7368-6496-2 (hardcover)
ISBN-13: 978-0-7368-7532-5 (softcover pbk.)
ISBN-10: 0-7368-7532-8 (softcover pbk.)
1. Earhart, Amelia, 1897–1937—Juvenile literature. 2. Air pilots—United States—Biography—Juvenile literature. 3. Women air pilots—United States—Biography—Juvenile literature. I. Whigham, Rod, 1954– II. Barnett, Charles, III. III. Title. IV. Series.
TL540.E3A75 2007
629.13092—dc22 2006004135

Summary: In graphic novel format, tells the story of Amelia Earhart, the daring female aviator who disappeared while attempting to become the first woman to pilot a plane around the world.

Art Direction and Design
Bob Lentz

Production Artist
Rana Raeuchle

Colorist
Matt Webb

Editor
Christine Peterson

Editor's note: Direct quotations from primary sources are indicated by a yellow background.

Direct quotations appear on the following pages:
Page 17, from a 1928 *New York Times* article written by Amelia Earhart, as published in *East to the Dawn: The Life of Amelia Earhart* by Susan Butler (Reading, Mass.: Addison-Wesley, 1997).
Pages 26 and 27, from the July 2, 1937, radio logs of the U.S. Coast Guard ship *Itasca* as transcribed by The International Group for Historic Aircraft Recovery (TIGHAR) (http://www.tighar.org/Projects/Earhart/Bulletins/37_ItascaLogs/Itascalog.html).

TABLE
of
Contents

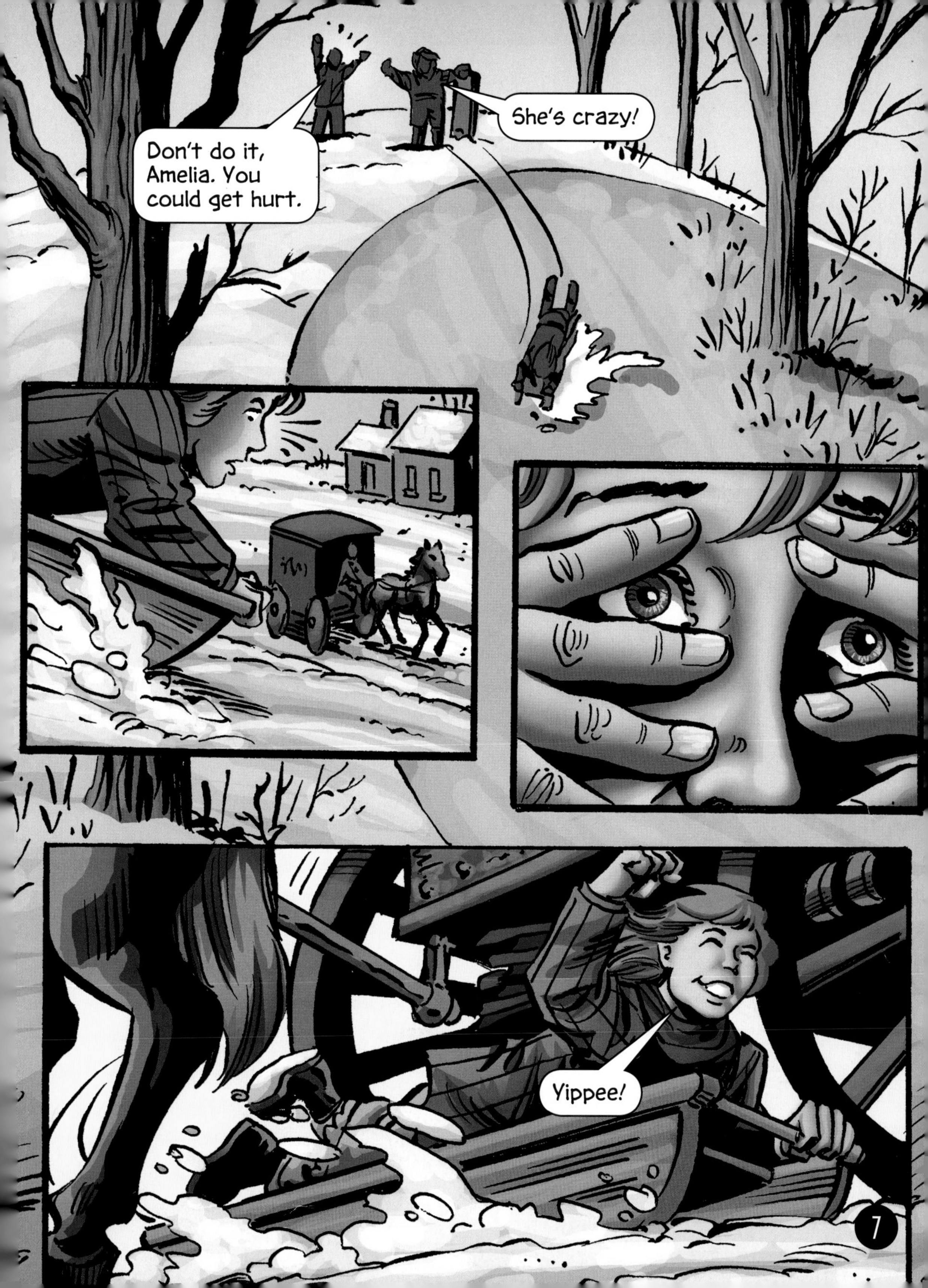
Don't do it, Amelia. You could get hurt.
She's crazy!
Yippee!

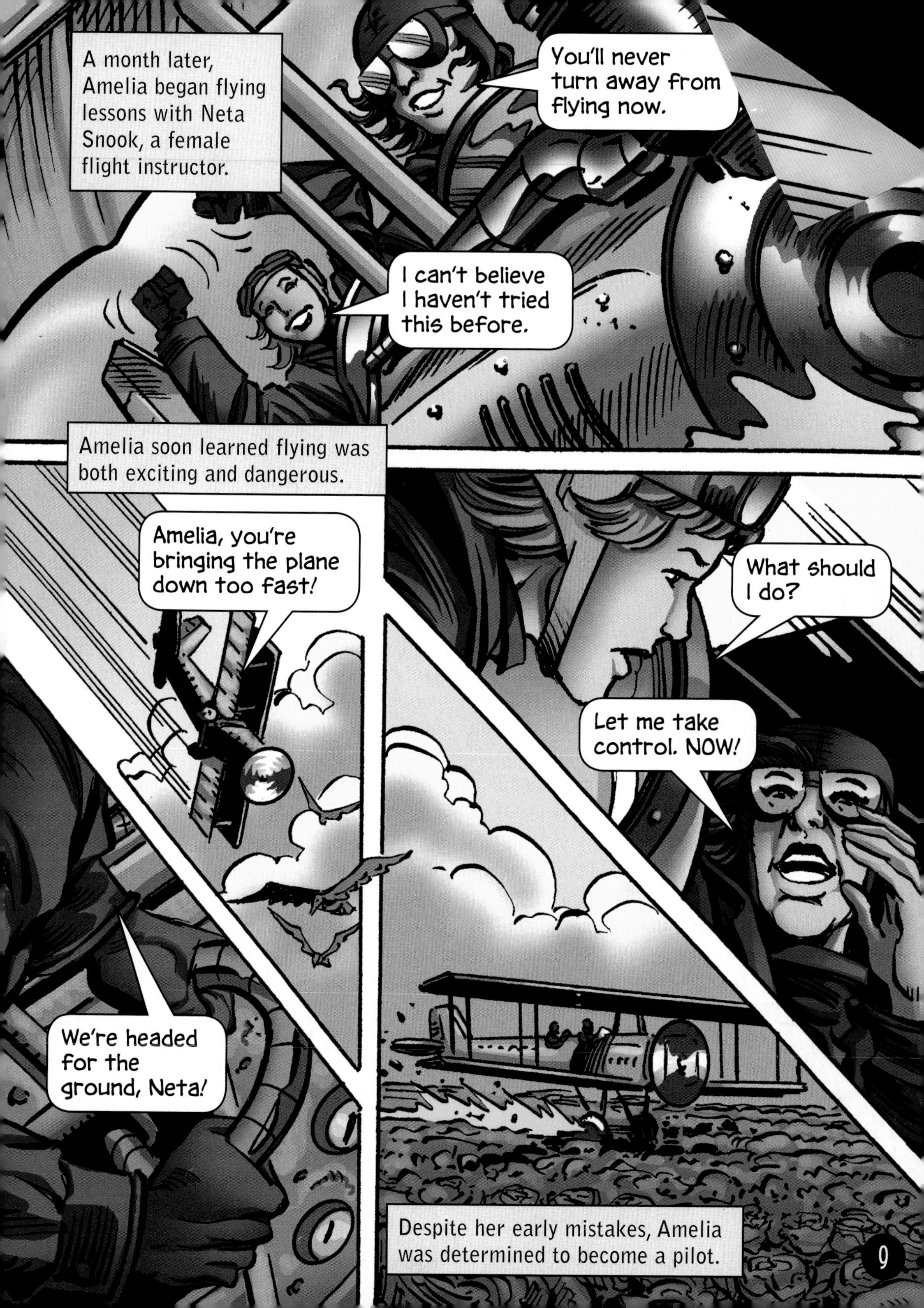
A month later, Amelia began flying lessons with Neta Snook, a female flight instructor.
You'll never turn away from flying now.
I can't believe I haven't tried this before.
Amelia soon learned flying was both exciting and dangerous.
Amelia, you're bringing the plane down too fast!
What should I do?
Let me take control. NOW!
We're headed for the ground, Neta!
Despite her early mistakes, Amelia was determined to become a pilot.

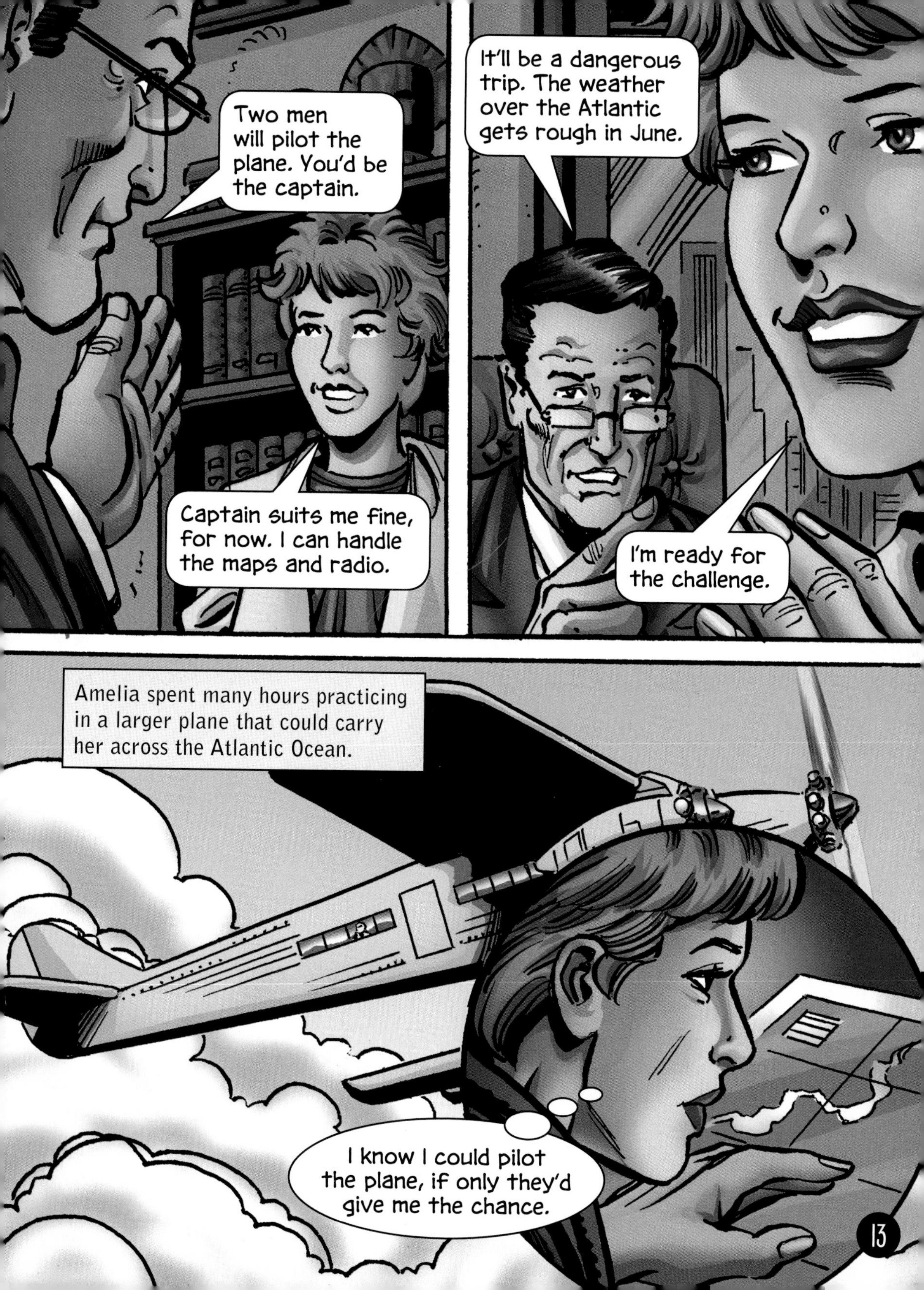
Two men will pilot the plane. You'd be the captain.
Captain suits me fine, for now. I can handle the maps and radio.
It'll be a dangerous trip. The weather over the Atlantic gets rough in June.
I'm ready for the challenge.
Amelia spent many hours practicing in a larger plane that could carry her across the Atlantic Ocean.
I know I could pilot the plane, if only they'd give me the chance.

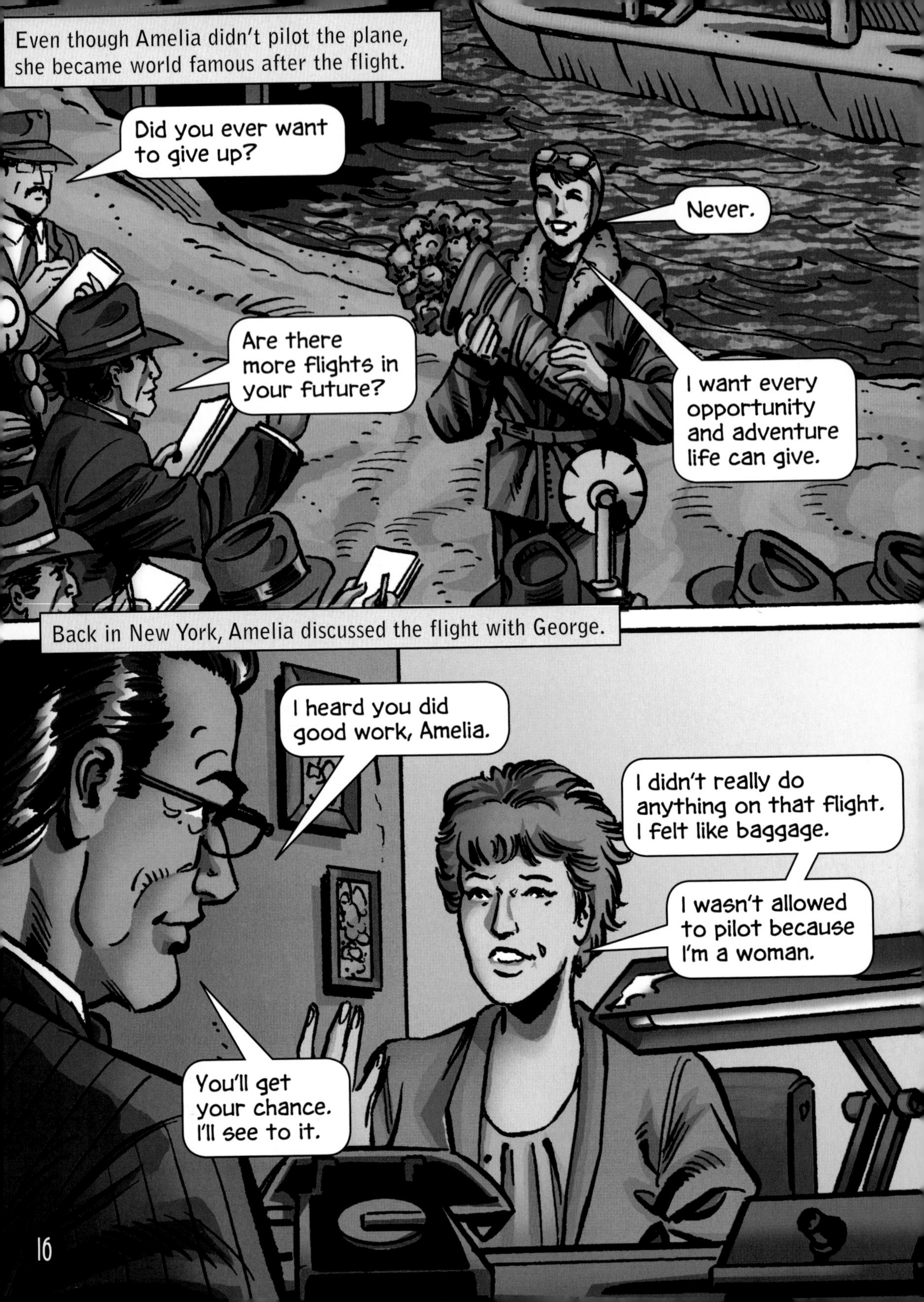
Even though Amelia didn't pilot the plane, she became world famous after the flight.
Did you ever want to give up?
Never.
Are there more flights in your future?
I want every opportunity and adventure life can give.
Back in New York, Amelia discussed the flight with George.
I heard you did good work, Amelia.
I didn't really do anything on that flight. I felt like baggage.
I wasn't allowed to pilot because I'm a woman.
You'll get your chance. I'll see to it.

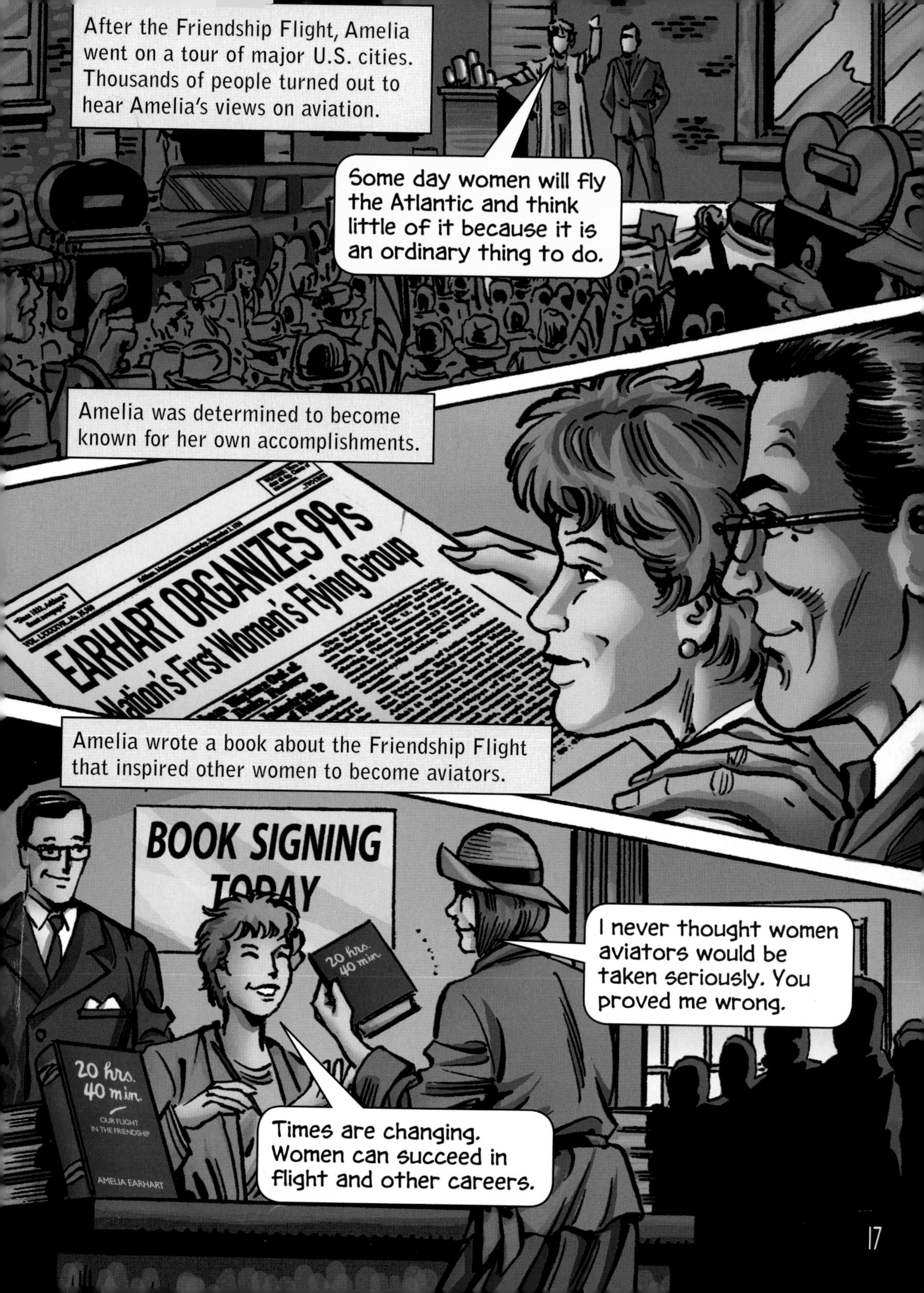
After the Friendship Flight, Amelia went on a tour of major U.S. cities. Thousands of people turned out to hear Amelia's views on aviation.
Some day women will fly the Atlantic and think little of it because it is an ordinary thing to do.
Amelia was determined to become known for her own accomplishments.
EARHART ORGANIZES 99s
Nation's First Women's Flying Group
Amelia wrote a book about the Friendship Flight that inspired other women to become aviators.
BOOK SIGNING TODAY
20 hrs. 40 min.
I never thought women aviators would be taken seriously. You proved me wrong.
20 hrs. 40 min.
OUR FLIGHT IN THE FRIENDSHIP
AMELIA EARHART
Times are changing. Women can succeed in flight and other careers.

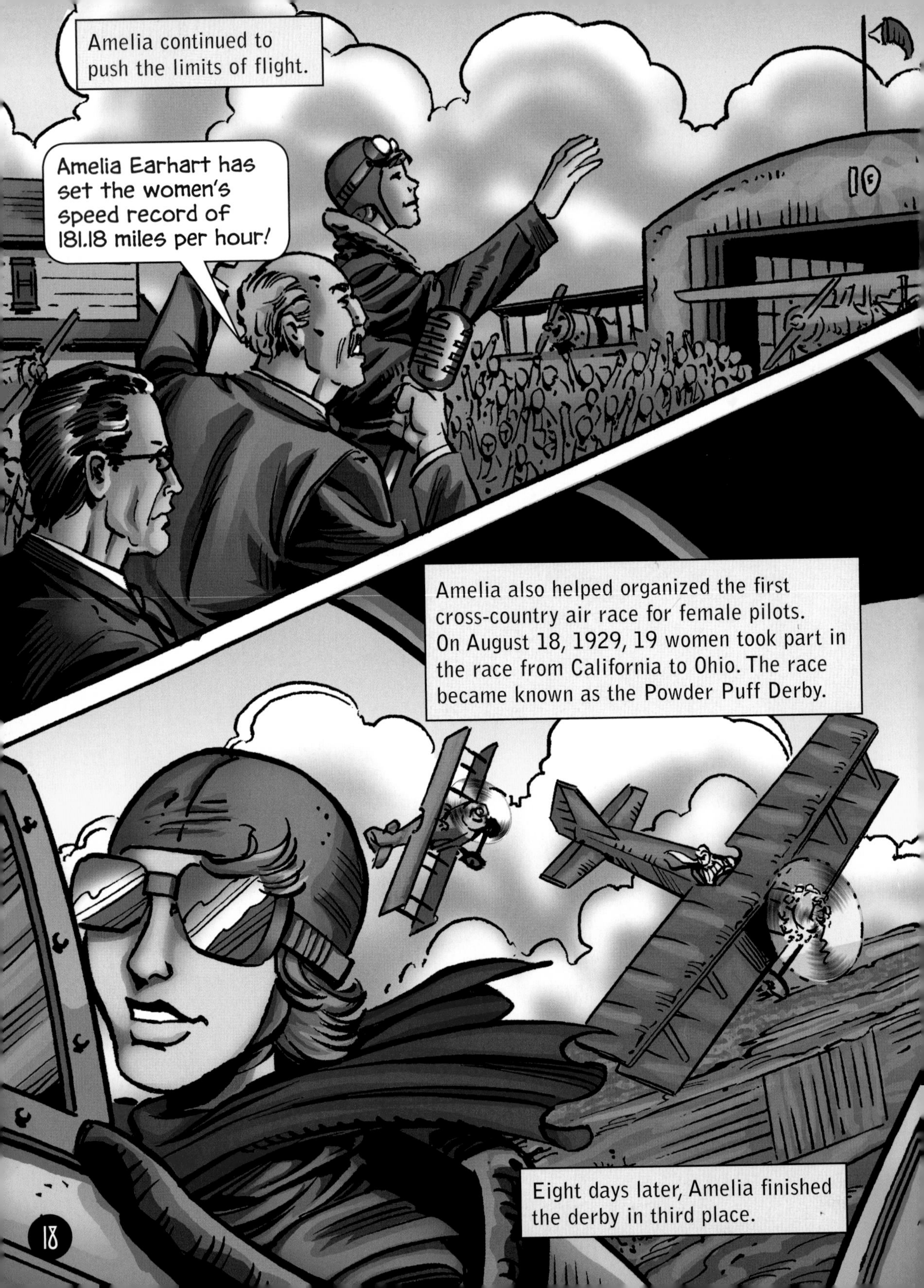
Amelia continued to push the limits of flight.
Amelia Earhart has set the women's speed record of 181.18 miles per hour!
Amelia also helped organized the first cross-country air race for female pilots. On August 18, 1929, 19 women took part in the race from California to Ohio. The race became known as the Powder Puff Derby.
Eight days later, Amelia finished the derby in third place.

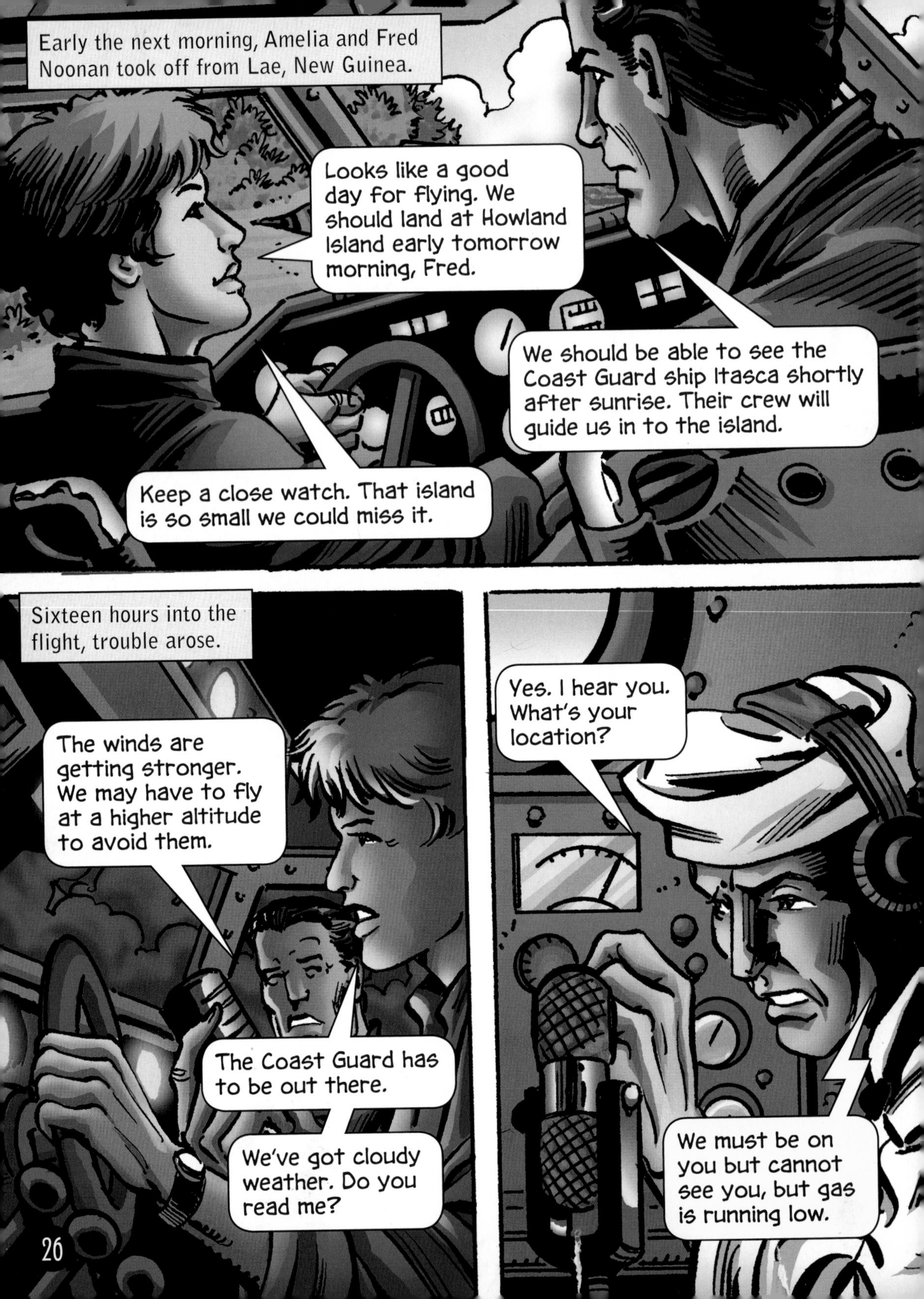
Early the next morning, Amelia and Fred Noonan took off from Lae, New Guinea.
Looks like a good day for flying. We should land at Howland Island early tomorrow morning, Fred.
We should be able to see the Coast Guard ship Itasca shortly after sunrise. Their crew will guide us in to the island.
Keep a close watch. That island is so small we could miss it.
Sixteen hours into the flight, trouble arose.
The winds are getting stronger. We may have to fly at a higher altitude to avoid them.
The Coast Guard has to be out there.
We've got cloudy weather. Do you read me?
Yes. I hear you. What's your location?
We must be on you but cannot see you, but gas is running low.

Amelia and Fred were never heard from again. Amelia's plane was never found. No one knows what happened during the last hours of Amelia's final flight.

Today, Amelia lives on as a legend of flight. She remains an inspiration to pilots everywhere.

AMELIA EARHART

- Amelia Earhart was born July 24, 1897, in Atchison, Kansas.

- Amelia saw her first airplane at a fair in Iowa. "It's just rusty wire and wood. It's not at all interesting," she said.

- It took Amelia 14 hours and 54 minutes to cross the Atlantic Ocean during her solo flight. Today, planes can make that same trip in about seven hours.

- Amelia's solo flight across the Atlantic was very dangerous. At one point, a broken piece of an engine ring caught on fire. The fire went out, but not before it damaged the metal of Amelia's plane.

- Amelia wrote three books about her aviation career. Her book *20 hrs. 40 min.* tells the story of the Friendship Flight. In *For the Fun of It*, Amelia writes about her love for adventure and flight. Her final book, *Last Flight*, was published by her husband shortly after Amelia disappeared. This book includes accounts of Amelia's final flight up until she and Fred left Lae, New Guinea.

- In 1931, Amelia became the first president of the Ninety Nines, a women's flying group that is still active today.

After Amelia's plane went missing, the U.S. government spent $4 million on the search for her, Fred, and their airplane.

People have come up with many ideas about what happened to Amelia on her final flight. Some believe Amelia's Lockheed Electra ran out of gas and crashed into the Pacific Ocean, killing Amelia and Fred. Others think that the plane crashed on a nearby island. Still others believe that after the Electra crashed, Amelia and Fred were captured by Japanese soldiers and treated as spies or possibly killed.

Amelia left behind a letter explaining her love of flight. "Please know I am quite aware of the hazards. I want to do it because I want to do it. Women must try to do things as men have tried. When they fail, their failure must be but a challenge to others."

GLOSSARY

altitude (AL-ti-tood)—the height of an object above the ground

aviator (AY-vee-ay-tur)—a person who flies an airplane

bearings (BAIR-ingz)—your sense of direction in relation to where things are

gauges (GAY-jiz)—the instruments used to measure information such as speed

mechanic (muh-KAN-ik)—someone who fixes vehicles or machinery

navigator (NAV-uh-gay-tuhr)—someone who plans an airplane's flight path; navigators read maps for pilots.

INTERNET SITES

FactHound offers a safe, fun way to find Internet sites related to this book. All of the sites on FactHound have been researched by our staff.

Here's how:
1. Visit *www.facthound.com*
2. Choose your grade level.
3. Type in this book ID **0736864962** for age-appropriate sites. You may also browse subjects by clicking on letters, or by clicking on pictures and words.
4. Click on the **Fetch It** button.

FactHound will fetch the best sites for you!

READ MORE

Klingel, Cynthia Fitterer. *Amelia Earhart: Aviation Pioneer.* Our People. Chanhassen, Minn.: Child's World, 2004.

McLeese, Don. *Amelia Earhart.* Discover the Life of an American Legend. Vero Beach, Fla.: Rourke, 2002.

Micklos, John. *Unsolved: What Really Happened to Amelia Earhart?* Prime. Berkeley Heights, N.J.: Enslow, 2006.

O'Brien, Patrick. *Fantastic Flights: One Hundred Years of Flying on the Edge.* New York: Walker & Company, 2003.

BIBLIOGRAPHY

Butler, Susan. *East to the Dawn: The Life of Amelia Earhart.* Reading, Mass.: Addison-Wesley, 1997.

Earhart, Amelia. *20 hrs. 40 min.: Our Flight in the Friendship.* New York: G. P. Putnam's Sons, 1928.

Earhart, Amelia. *Last Flight.* New York: Harcourt, Brace, 1937.

Putnam, George Palmer. *Soaring Wings: A Biography of Amelia Earhart.* New York: Harcourt, Brace, and Company, 1939.

INDEX